RAIN FOREST FOOD CHAINS

Heidi Moore

Heinemann
LIBRARY

Chicago, Illinois

www.heinemannraintree.com
Visit our website to find out more information about Heinemann-Raintree books.

To order:
☎ Phone 888-454-2279
💻 Visit www.heinemannraintree.com to browse our catalog and order online.

©2011 Heinemann Library
an imprint of Capstone Global Library, LLC
Chicago, Illinois

Edited by Abby Colich and Andrew Farrow
Designed by Victoria Allen
Illustrated by Words and Publications
Picture research by Mica Brancic
Originated by Capstone Global Library, Ltd.
Printed by China Translation & Printing Services, Ltd.

14 13 12 11 10
10 9 8 7 6 5 4 3 2 1

Library of Congress Cataloging-in-Publication Data
Moore, Heidi, 1976-
   Rain forest food chains / Heidi Moore.
       p. cm. -- (Protecting food chains)
   Includes bibliographical references and index.
   ISBN 978-1-4329-3860-4 (hc) -- ISBN 978-1-4329-3867-3 (pb) 1. Rain forest ecology--Juvenile literature. 2. Food chains (Ecology)--Juvenile literature. I. Title.
   QH541.5.R27M66 2011
   577.34'16--dc22
                                     2009049548

Acknowledgments
Corbis pp. 29 (©Kevin Schafer), 40 (epa/©How Hwee Young); FLPA p. 42 (Frans Lanting); Getty Images pp. 13 (Photolibrary), 26 (National Geographic/Joel Sartore), 33 (National Geographic/Timothy Laman), 41 (National Geographic/Randy Olson), 43 (The Image Bank/Simon Rawles); Photolibrary pp. 4 (age fotostock/Berndt Fischer), 8 (Oxford Scientific (OSF)/Edward Parker), 14 (Animals Animals/Fabio Colombini Medeiros), 15 (Japan Travel Bureau/JTB Photo), 17 (Oxford Scientific (OSF)), 18 (All Canada Photos/Glenn Bartley), 19 (Picture Press/J & C Sohns), 22 (Oxford Scientific (OSF)/Stan Osolinski), 23 (age fotostock/Andoni Canela), 25 (Oxford Scientific (OSF)/Carol Farneti Foster), 27 (Oxford Scientific (OSF)/Rob Nunnington), 28 (Oxford Scientific (OSF)/Roy Toft), 31 (Oxford Scientific (OSF)/Nick Gordon), 34 (Oxford Scientific (OSF)/Patricio Robles Gil), 35 (Loren McIntyre), 36 (imagebroker.net/Heiner Heine), 37 (age fotostock/Andoni Canela), 38 (Animals Animals/Nigel JH Smith); Photoshot p. 21 (©NHPA/Daniel Heuclin); Shutterstock pp. 9 (©Juriah Mosin), 39 (Ralph Loesche).

Cover photograph of an orangutan (Pongo pygmaeus) in Tanjung Puting National Park, Central-Kalimantan, Borneo, Indonesia, reproduced with permission of Photolibrary (imagebroker.net/ROM ROM).

Cover and spread background image reproduced with permission of Shutterstock (©Clearviewstock).

We would like to thank Kenneth Dunton and Dana Sjostrom for their invaluable help in the preparation of this book.

Every effort has been made to contact copyright holders of any material reproduced in this book. Any omissions will be rectified in subsequent printings if notice is given to the publisher.

CONTENTS

What Is a Rain Forest Food Chain? 4

What Is a Rain Forest Habitat? 8

Where in the World Are Rain Forest Habitats? 10

What Are the Producers in Rain Forests? 12

What Are the Primary Consumers in Rain Forests?.....................16

What Are the Secondary Consumers in Rain Forests? 20

What Are the Decomposers in Rain Forests?...............................24

What Are Rain Forest Food Chains Like Around the World?.......28

How Are Humans Harming Rain Forest Food Chains?.................34

What Can You Do to Protect Rain Forest Food Chains?.............40

Top 10 Things You Can Do to Protect Rain Forests....................44

Glossary..45

Find Out More...47

Index..48

Some words are shown in bold, **like this**. You can find out what they mean by looking in the glossary.

WHAT IS A RAIN FOREST FOOD CHAIN?

The warm, moist Amazon River **basin** is home to the world's largest rain forest. Part the dense **vegetation** (plant life) and take a peek. Thousands of different plants and animals live here, between the damp ground and the treetops.

On the forest floor, a millipede munches a leaf. Soon a furry brown wolf spider inches closer. It traps the millipede and gobbles it up. Suddenly a brightly colored toucan leaves its treetop perch. Toucans mostly eat berries and seeds, but today it spies the wolf spider and glides down toward it. The toucan snatches the spider in its beak and swallows it whole.

When the toucan dies, **decomposers** such as **bacteria** will break down its body. Decomposers break down dead plant and animal material. This releases **energy** back into the water and soil. Soon other living things will take in that energy, and the process will begin again.

An orangutan crouches in the dense rain forest vegetation.

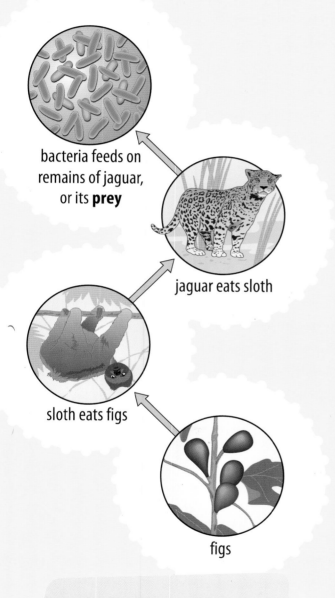

bacteria feeds on remains of jaguar, or its **prey**

jaguar eats sloth

sloth eats figs

figs

This food chain diagram shows how energy moves from one organism to another.

FOOD CHAINS

This process is called a food chain. A food chain shows how energy moves from one **organism** to another. An organism is any living thing. Energy moves from one living thing to another when one organism feeds on another.

Sometimes this process is shown using a food chain diagram. A food chain diagram has a series of arrows. The arrows show the flow of energy. Energy flows from the food to the animal that eats it. For example, in the rain forest food chain to the left, the arrow leads from the figs to the sloth, from the sloth to the jaguar, and so on.

Each link in a food chain is important. When something happens to one link, it affects the entire chain. Although humans have done much to harm rain forest food chains, they depend on them, too. It is important that humans start working to protect Earth's rain forests.

WHAT ARE THE PARTS OF A FOOD CHAIN?

Producers are plants. Plants use light energy from the Sun to produce food.

A **consumer** cannot make its own food. Consumers eat plants, animals, or both. There are three types of consumer. A **primary consumer**, or **herbivore**, eats only plants. **Carnivores** eat only animals. **Omnivores** eat both plants and animals. Carnivores and omnivores are also called **secondary consumers**.

Decomposers help release energy for producers. This frees up energy for the food chain process to continue. Decomposers feed on matter that is decaying, or breaking down.

You may have heard the terms "**predator**" and "prey." A predator is an animal that eats another animal. The prey is the animal that is eaten. Food chains include both predators and prey.

Can an animal be both predator and prey? Yes. An animal might have two different roles in a food chain. Sometimes it might be a predator and eat smaller animals. But it might become prey when an animal higher up on the food chain eats it. One animal also can have a place in several food chains.

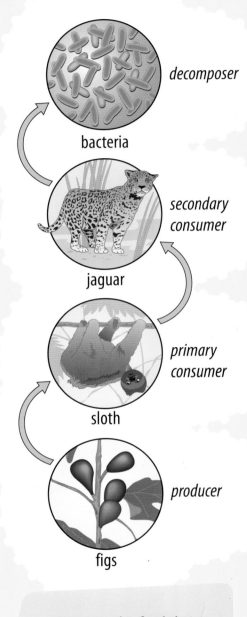

decomposer

bacteria

secondary consumer

jaguar

primary consumer

sloth

producer

figs

Energy in this food chain begins with a producer (fig) and ends with a decomposer (bacteria).

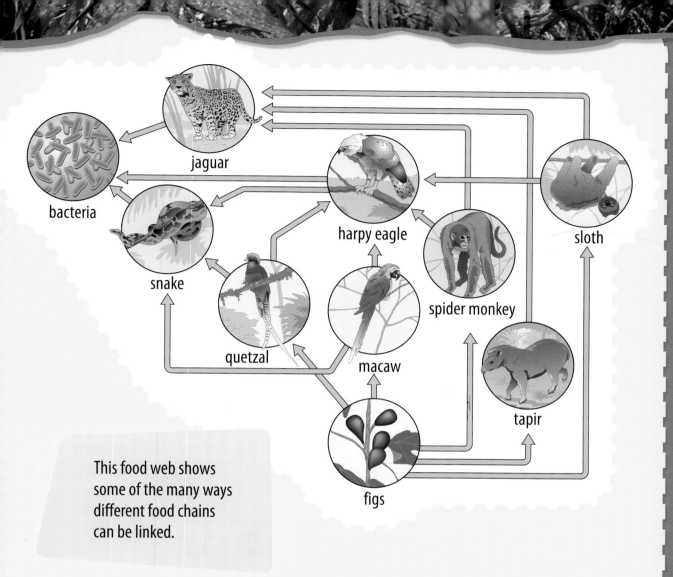

bacteria

jaguar

snake

harpy eagle

sloth

quetzal

macaw

spider monkey

figs

tapir

This food web shows some of the many ways different food chains can be linked.

WHAT IS A FOOD WEB?

Food chains only tell one part of the story. They show one series of links. Many organisms eat more than one type of organism. This is a good idea for survival. Animals that eat only one thing are at risk if something happens to their food source.

A food web shows how food chains are linked together. It looks a bit like a spider web. A food web shows how energy moves from organism to organism. It tells you who eats whom. In the food web above, figs are food for both tapirs and macaws.

WHAT IS A RAIN FOREST HABITAT?

Rain forests are warm areas of dense **vegetation** and heavy rain. The hot, moist conditions support many different **species** (types) of plants and animals. You can find rain forests in **tropical** areas all over the world. The largest rain forests are in South America around the Amazon River, in Africa around the Congo and Niger rivers, and in India and Southeast Asia. Australia, the Philippines, and Papua New Guinea also have smaller rain forests.

The rain forest is an amazing place to live. It is very warm all year long. The temperature usually stays between 20°C (68°F) and 32°C (90°F). Within each rain forest are many different **habitats**. A habitat is a place where **organisms** of the same kind live. Organisms depend on their habitat for food, shelter, water, and everything else they need to survive.

The Korup National Rain Forest in Cameroon sustains a wide variety of organisms.

HOW MUCH RAIN?

Between 150 centimeters (60 inches) and 1,000 centimeters (390 inches) of rain fall in rain forests each year.

Red and blue macaws rest on the branch of a rain forest tree.

The top layer of the rain forest is called the **canopy**. It is a dense group of treetops, forming a blanket of leaves. Sometimes the canopy is so dense it does not allow sunlight to get through. Below the canopy, the **understory** is alive with climbing animals, tangling vines, and flowering orchids. On the forest floor, deer **graze**, army ants march, and ferns and mosses grow.

All living things are **adapted** to their habitat. If a plant lives in the canopy and needs lots of sunlight, then it is adapted to the canopy. It likely would not survive on the forest floor. Over time organisms develop **adaptations** that help them survive in certain habitats.

WHERE IN THE WORLD ARE RAIN FOREST HABITATS?

The map below shows the location of the world's rain forests.

NORTH
AMERICA

Central American
rain forest

Amazon rain forest

SOUTH
AMERICA

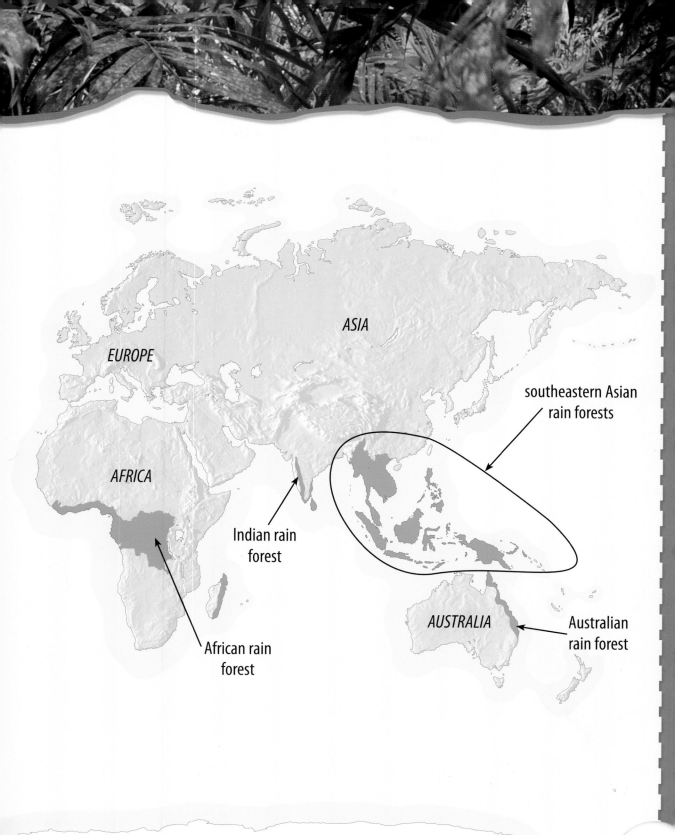

EUROPE

ASIA

AFRICA

southeastern Asian
rain forests

Indian rain
forest

African rain
forest

AUSTRALIA

Australian
rain forest

WHAT ARE THE PRODUCERS IN RAIN FORESTS?

Producers, or plants, turn **energy** from the Sun into food. This process is called **photosynthesis**.

All producers need sunlight, water, carbon dioxide, and **nutrients** to grow. Plants contain **chlorophyll**, a substance that makes them green. Chlorophyll is made of protein that helps plants trap sunlight to use in photosynthesis.

Producers are very important. All **consumers** depend on producers in some way. Some consumers eat producers. Some eat other consumers that eat producers. If the producers disappeared, the consumers would, too. It would affect the entire food chain.

PLANT LAYERS

Producers live at different layers of the rain forest. Tall evergreen trees reach 23 to 30 meters (75 to 100 feet) to form the **canopy**. That is about as high as 13 to 16 people standing on each other's shoulders. Some very tall trees poke through this high canopy. This is called the **emergent layer**.

Below the canopy is the **understory**. This is where smaller trees, plants, and shrubs grow. On the forest floor is a layer of ferns, mosses, and herbs.

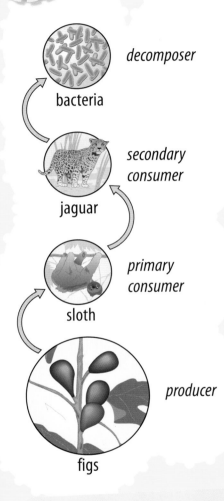

decomposer
bacteria

secondary consumer
jaguar

primary consumer
sloth

producer

figs

Producers such as the fig get energy from the Sun before being eaten by a consumer.

STRANGLER FIGS

Some plants have unusual ways of taking in nutrients. Strangler figs are able to draw out nutrients from trees. Wind blows strangler fig seeds onto a treetop. From its treetop perch, it grows roots down the tree. These roots take in nutrients from the tree. Eventually a strangler fig kills its host tree by squeezing its trunk and sucking out all of its nutrients.

The strangler fig's roots take in nutrients from the tree it grows on.

WHAT PLANTS CAN BE FOUND IN RAIN FORESTS?

Rain forest soil does not contain many nutrients. Plants **adapt** to get nutrients from ground plants that die and decay. The dead matter settles in the top layer of soil. Trees and plants take in these nutrients through shallow roots.

Thick green or woody vines are a common sight in the rain forest. Vines are plants that attach to other plants. They climb up trees to catch the sunlight. But vines also serve another function. Monkeys and orangutans use them to travel from tree to tree!

A bromeliad's waxy leaves are good at trapping water.

AIR PLANTS

Some of the most unusual rain forest plants are **epiphytes**. Epiphytes are air plants that have adapted to living above the soil. They grow on tree trunks or branches. But they do not take in nutrients from the tree. They absorb nutrients right from the air and rainwater. Epiphytes include mosses, lichens, orchids, ferns, and bromeliads.

Orchids and bromeliads bring bursts of color to the rain forest. Many orchids have striking, colorful blooms. Bromeliads' thick, waxy leaves form a bowl to collect water. Sometimes insects or tiny frogs live in this pool of water!

LOSING A LINK: HEALING PLANTS

The Amazon rain forest has tens of thousands of plant **species**. Some of these plants can be used as medicine. There are rain forest plants that cure malaria and some that help fight cancer. Many of these special plants cannot be found anywhere else in the world. Scientists believe many species of healing plants have not been discovered yet. But **habitat** loss is putting these species at risk. Many are dying out before scientists have a chance to find them. When species die out, we lose chances to save lives.

Bark from the cinchona tree can be used to make a medicine that fights malaria.

WHAT ARE THE PRIMARY CONSUMERS IN RAIN FORESTS?

Any **organism** above the level of **producer** is a **consumer**. Consumers cannot make their own food. They feed on producers or other consumers. Right above the producers in the food chain are the **primary** (first) **consumers**. Primary consumers feed on producers. They are **herbivores**, or plant-eaters.

Many different primary consumers live in the rain forest. There is a wide range of plant **species** to support them. Some organisms remain in the **canopy** their entire lives. Others remain on the forest floor. Rain forest primary consumers include insects, butterflies, birds, and rodents.

REMARKABLE RODENTS

One of the largest rain forest rodents is the agouti. Agoutis look like large guinea pigs. They have coarse, oily hair, small ears, and a stumpy tail. They live in burrows or hollow tree trunks and eat fallen fruit and nuts.

The world's largest rodent is the capybara. The piglike creature has shaggy, reddish-brown fur. It lives in South America and grows up to 0.6 meters (2 feet) tall. Capybaras feed mainly on grasses, water plants, and fruit. Sometimes they eat their own **feces** (poo)! The poop contains **bacteria** that help break down tough plant material in the capybara's stomach.

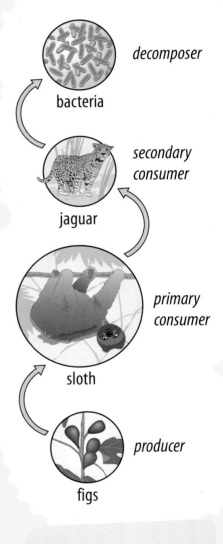

decomposer
bacteria

secondary consumer
jaguar

primary consumer
sloth

producer
figs

The sloth, a primary consumer, feeds on figs, a producer.

Rain forest ants climb an acacia plant. The ants live in the hollow thorns.

PERFECT PARTNERS

Ants have a special relationship with the acacia plant. Hollow acacia thorns provide shelter and food for ants and their young. The ants, in turn, protect the acacia from organisms that try to eat it.

SLOW AS A SLOTH

The three-toed sloth lives in Central and South America. It clings to trees with its clawed feet. It moves so slowly that algae grows on its shaggy fur. This helps it blend in with rain forest **vegetation** and avoid **predators**. The three-toed sloth sleeps up to 20 hours a day. Leaves and twigs make up its diet.

RAIN FOREST FLIERS

Many flying creatures make their home in the rain forest. These include bats, birds, and butterflies.

BATS

Fruit bats are an important part of the rain forest food chain. Some plants depend on the bat for **pollination** (fertilization). When a bat drinks **nectar** from a flower, it also **pollinates** the flower.

BIRDS

The rain forest is alive with bird sounds. Toucans boast colorful bills and black and yellow bodies. They eat fruit, insects, small lizards, and eggs. They can warm up or cool down their bills to control their body temperature.

Noisy parrots live in rain forests around the world. They fly from treetop to treetop in the canopy and **emergent layer**. Their sharp beaks break apart nuts, seeds, and fruits.

Hummingbirds are the smallest birds on Earth. They beat their wings so fast you can barely see them. They hover in midair and dip their long beaks into the sweet nectar of a flower, sucking it up with their long tongues.

A hummingbird feeds on sweet nectar in midair.

BUTTERFLIES

More species of butterflies live in the rain forest than anywhere else. The Amazon rain forest alone contains 7,500 species.

The blue morpho butterfly has striking blue wings. Actually, the wings are not colored blue. Tiny scales on top of the wings reflect blue light, making them appear blue. With its wings closed, the dull brown underside shows. This makes it hard for predators, such as birds, to see it. Adult blue morphos sip tree sap and fruit juice.

Scales on top of the blue morpho butterfly's wings reflect blue light.

A Broken Chain: Fruit Bats

In Queensland, Australia, fruit bats are at risk. Because of **habitat** loss, they cannot find enough **pollen** and nectar from their usual plant sources. So they head lower into the **understory** to eat wild tobacco berries. But this plant is home to a deadly tick that has killed many bats. Without fruit bats to pollinate them, many rain forest plants could die out.

WHAT ARE THE SECONDARY CONSUMERS IN RAIN FORESTS?

Secondary consumers feed on **primary consumers**. These **predators** hunt and eat other animals.

GROUND PREDATORS

Rain forest ground predators include snakes, lizards, and small **mammals** such as bandicoots and coatimundi. Mammals are furry, warm-blooded animals that produce milk to feed their young.

Most rain forest snakes are small to medium in size and **prey** on insects, birds, and small mammals. The giant anaconda can grow up to 9 meters (30 feet) long. Found in South America and Trinidad, it is one of the world's largest snakes. These big snakes eat a wide range of animals, including deer, turtles, fish, and birds.

Australian bandicoots have long, pointed noses like rodents, but are not rodents. They forage at night for worms, spiders, insects, and plant roots. Bandicoots nest on the ground or in hollow logs.

The coatimundi are related to raccoons. They have thick fur and use a long tail for balance. Coatimundis search for food on the forest floor and in the **understory**. They are **omnivores**. They eat scorpions, spiders, lizards, rodents and small mammals. They also eat fruit. In fact, coatis eat just about anything!

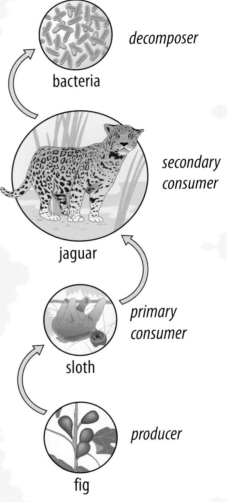

decomposer
bacteria

secondary consumer
jaguar

primary consumer
sloth

producer
fig

The jaguar, a secondary consumer, eats primary consumers such as a sloth.

Not all snakes stick to slithering. Snakes such as this Chrysopelea appear to fly when they glide through the air.

FLYING PREDATORS

Some predators have special **adaptations** to get from tree to tree. They look as if they fly, but they do not have wings. Insect-eating frogs use webbed feet to glide short distances between trees. Flying snakes of the Southeast Asian rain forest glide from tree to tree in search of their prey— mostly birds, bats, rodents, and lizards. The flying dragon is a rain forest lizard that eats insects. It stretches its skin so that it can sail between trees up to 8 meters (25 feet) apart.

TOP RAIN FOREST CONSUMERS

The rain forest food web contains many **primate species**. Primates are a group of mammals that share certain features. They have hands that grasp and well-formed brains. Monkeys and gorillas are primates. So are humans. Some primates are primary consumers, and some are secondary consumers. Both chimpanzees and mandrills are secondary consumers.

Chimpanzees are humans' closest relatives. Like humans, they are omnivores. They eat fruits and vegetables and some animals, including insects, monkeys, and pigs. Chimps can use tools. They poke long sticks and branches into termites' nests to get at the tasty snack.

Shy monkey-like mandrills are difficult to spot in the wild. They live in **tropical** African rain forests. Mandrills eat reptiles and insects as well as roots and fruits. They live in groups, and the males have colorful faces.

Chimpanzees use twigs to dig into trees for termites.

TOP RAIN FOREST PREDATORS

Do any creatures feed on secondary consumers? Yes. These are the top predators in the rain forest food chain. They are fearsome **carnivores**. Some call them **tertiary consumers**, meaning "third-level **consumers**."

The top rain forest predators are the "big cats," such as jaguars and ocelots. Fierce jaguars prey on tapirs, monkeys, tortoises, and birds. Ocelots are not very big—about twice the size of a pet cat—but they are good hunters. Their sharp teeth tear into rabbits, rodents, frogs, and other small animals.

MOST DANGEROUS PREDATOR

Another top predator is . . . you! Humans hunted big cats almost to **extinction**. In some parts of the world, people hunt and eat chimps and other primates. Laws are in place to protect these animals, but some people ignore the laws.

An ocelot is on the prowl for prey.

LOSING A LINK: BIG CATS IN DANGER

Top predators need large ranges, or areas of land to hunt in. As rain forest **habitat** disappears, it is harder for the big cats to survive. Many are now **endangered**, or at risk of dying out.

WHAT ARE THE DECOMPOSERS IN RAIN FORESTS?

Decomposers are an important link in the rain forest food chain. They play a key role in the cycle of life and death. Decomposers break down dead plant and animal matter. This frees up **nutrients** for the beginning of the chain. Then rain forest **producers** consume these nutrients, and the food chain begins again.

This process is a bit like recycling. When we put out glass bottles to be recycled, the glass can be used again to make other things. When decomposers break down matter, it can be used again. This is especially important in the rain forest, where the soil is poor. Plants take in nutrients directly from decaying matter.

Without decomposers, the waste would build up and up and up. Soon the entire rain forest would be filled with dead matter.

In this food chain, a decomposer (bacteria) breaks down the body of a **secondary consumer** (jaguar).

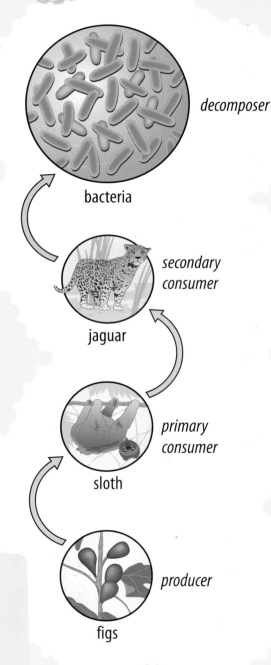

decomposer

bacteria

secondary consumer

jaguar

primary consumer

sloth

producer

figs

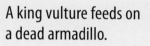

A king vulture feeds on a dead armadillo.

SCAVENGER HUNT

Scavengers begin the process of breaking down dead matter. Termites help break down fallen trees and branches. Worms go to work on dead plants and animals. Dung beetles eat rotting fruit and leaves as well as **feces**.

King vultures are the bird world's largest scavengers. They soar above the **canopy** looking for dead animals to feast on. The vulture's yucky diet might help out in another way. Eating rotting animal flesh might help stop the spread of disease.

Long trails of leaf-cutter ants are common sights in rain forests. These ants do not actually feed on leaves. They feed on a **fungus** that grows on piling up leaf material. They cut up leaves into smaller pieces to bring back to their colony. There, the fungus breaks down the leaf pieces. Leaf-cutter ants are very strong. They can carry leaf pieces 20 times their weight. A person who could do that would be able to lift a small car!

BREAKING IT DOWN

Rain forests are areas of high temperatures and lots of moisture. This helps plant matter break down quickly. Dead plants and animals can break down as quickly as 24 hours in the rain forest if it is hot and moist enough. In other places, it can take far longer for material to break down. **Bacteria** and fungi complete the process of breaking down dead matter.

LOSING A LINK: FROG-KILLING FUNGUS

Most fungi are important rain forest decomposers. But one type of chytrid fungus is killing frogs in Australia and Central America. The fungus causes a deadly skin disease in some frogs. Many frogs have died out, and many more are at risk. Most types of chytrid fungi help break down plant matter. Scientists are not sure why one type became harmful to frogs.

This frog is being tested for a deadly fungus.

BENEFICIAL BACTERIA

Bacteria are the main rain forest decomposers. These are very simple but important **organisms**. Bacteria are single-celled organisms. (Cells are the smallest units of living things.) Some bacteria are shaped like rods, and others are spirals.

Bacteria are tiny. You could fit about a million of them on the head of a pin. Bacteria help break down dead matter into substances other organisms can use. Some bacteria live everywhere, including the digestive systems of rain forest organisms, helping them break down food. Other bacteria live on feces and help break it down.

FUNGUS AMONG US

Another important decomposer is fungus. Mushrooms are a common type of fungus. They grow especially well in warm, wet rain forests. Bracket fungi grow directly on dying or dead trees. They look like ladders attached to a tree trunk. Some fungi come in strange shapes. An earthstar puffball fungus looks like a puffy flower with spiky "petals."

These fungi acts as a decomposer of this dead rain forest tree.

WHAT ARE RAIN FOREST FOOD CHAINS LIKE AROUND THE WORLD?

Rain forest **habitats** share many features, but they are not all the same. **Species adapt** to their specific habitat. Rain forest food chains differ from one part of the world to another.

THE AMAZON RAIN FOREST

The Amazon River **basin** is home to the largest rain forest in the world. It stretches from Peru to eastern Brazil. The area contains almost half of the **tropical** rain forest habitat left in the world.

Nearly 40,000 plant species have been found here. The Amazon rain forest also boasts the most species of birds, butterflies, and freshwater fish on Earth.

A two-toed sloth rests on a branch in Costa Rica.

This pygmy marmoset lives on the trees in a rain forest in Brazil.

Jaguars prowl the forest floor looking for **prey**. Harpy eagles swoop down from above to tear into reptiles sunning on rocks. Two-toed sloths blend in with the dense **vegetation**. Colorful scarlet macaws squawk from their treetop perches.

Primates such as marmosets live in the lush **understory** of the Amazon. Tiny pygmy marmosets are the world's smallest monkeys. They grow to only 13 centimeters (5 inches) long. Marmosets feed on lizards, spiders, and insects as well as tree sap and fruit.

Poison dart frogs have a unique defense against **predators**. The colorful frogs release toxins (poison) from their skin. Predators that try to gobble up poison dart frogs get a painful—and sometimes deadly—surprise.

A BROKEN CHAIN: LOSING THE AMAZON

The Amazon is an important part of the planet. It is home to plants that can treat disease and save lives. Many animals found here cannot survive anywhere else. But the Amazon rain forest is disappearing. Farmers cut down and burn the edges of the rain forests to make room for crops and animals. Scientists say that more than half of the Amazon rain forest could be gone by 2030. Many plants and animals here are at risk of dying out.

THE AFRICAN RAIN FOREST

The African rain forest is the second largest in the world. It follows the path of Africa's Congo River. Half of all the animal species in Africa live in the rain forest.

Many of the **producers** here have practical uses. Coffee plants grow in the shade of tall trees. Local people harvest the pods of cacao trees to make chocolate. Wood from tall mahogany trees is used to make furniture and flooring. African oil palms produce oil for soap, chocolate, and other products.

The African rain forest is home to many primates, including lowland gorillas, chimpanzees, and bonobos. Bonobos, like chimps, are close relatives to humans. They feed on fruits, nuts, mushrooms, and sometimes rodents or small antelopes. Bonobos are found in the Congo and nowhere else on Earth.

Other rain forest **mammals** include forest elephants, hippopotamuses, and okapi. The okapi, a relative of the giraffe, lives only in the African rain forest. Okapis eat fruits, plants, and **fungi**. African elephants are one of the world's largest land animals. Adults eat up to 136 kilograms (300 pounds) of roots, fruits, grass, and bark each day.

This food chain shows one way plants and animals are consumed in the African rain forest.

stinkwood leaves

black-and-white colobus monkey

crowned hawk eagle

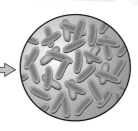
bacteria

A chimpanzee crouches in the West African rain forest.

LOSING A LINK: DISAPPEARING RAIN FORESTS

The African rain forest is disappearing—and along with it many primate species. Farming and road building are wiping out vast areas of land. Despite laws against it, some people still hunt and eat primates. About 90 percent of the African rain forest is gone already. What will happen to the primates?

GENTLE GIANTS

You might assume gorillas are tough predators. Think again. These powerful creatures look fierce but are actually quite gentle. They only strike out when threatened. Gorillas are mostly **herbivores** that eat leaves, shoots, and fruits.

SOUTHEAST ASIAN RAIN FOREST

In Southeast Asia, you will find the oldest rain forests in the world. These rain forests are not large expanses like those of the Amazon and Congo river basins. Thailand, Malaysia, and Myanmar (Burma) have smaller areas of rain forest. Sumatra, Borneo, New Guinea, and the Philippines also contain patches of rain forest. This is because the landscape contains many islands and because of human development.

All plants are producers. But some plants do double duty as **secondary consumers**, or **carnivores**! Pitcher plants have bowl-shaped parts that trap insects or other animals. The insect falls in or is lured in by sweet **nectar**. Then the pitcher plant takes in **nutrients** from the dead insect. Some pitcher plants in Southeast Asia lure in animals as large as rats!

Orangutans swing through the jungles of Sumatra and Borneo. The shaggy, red-haired apes spend most of their time in the understory. They munch on fruits, nuts, and bark. Sometimes birds' eggs or termites make tasty snacks for orangutans. About 50,000 orangutans remain in the wild. They are at risk of dying out.

Small lemurs live only on the island of Madagascar. They live in the trees and use their long, furry tails for balance. Some lemurs eat insects, while most eat leaves and fruit.

This food chain links organisms in the Southeast Asian rain forest.

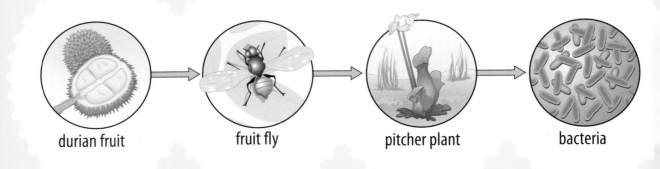

durian fruit   fruit fly   pitcher plant   bacteria

A Broken Chain: Borneo

The island of Borneo, which is a bit larger than the state of Texas, has an amazing number of species. About 15,000 species of plants are found here. Borneo's rain forest is the world's tallest. Many "flying" animals, from frogs and lizards to snakes and squirrels, fling themselves from tree to tree here. Today, less than half of Borneo's rain forest remains. Forest fires, logging, and farming have destroyed much of this unique habitat.

This Wallace's flying frog is found in the rain forest of the island of Borneo.

HOW ARE HUMANS HARMING RAIN FOREST FOOD CHAINS?

All over the world, rain forest food chains are in trouble. Human activity has already wiped out half of Earth's rain forests. Rain forests once covered 14 percent of Earth. Now they cover only 6 percent. Yet the rain forest is still home to half the **species** on Earth.

Why should we protect these special **habitats**? Rain forests house many rare plant and animal species. Many rain forest **organisms** cannot be found anywhere else on Earth. Some plant species can help treat or cure disease. When these species disappear, we lose chances to save lives.

LUNGS OF THE EARTH

Rain forests are like the lungs of the planet. They give off oxygen that humans and other animals need to breathe. They also act as a "carbon sink." Rain forest **vegetation** absorbs carbon dioxide gas. Otherwise, carbon dioxide would build up and trap heat, creating **global warming**. Global warming puts many species, including humans, at risk.

Rain forest plants absorb carbon dioxide and give off oxygen.

Burning can destroy
areas of rain forest.

HABITAT LOSS

From South America to Southeast Asia, rain forests are disappearing fast.
Every minute an area of rain forest the size of 50 football fields disappears.

Logging, farming, road building, and wars have led to widespread habitat loss.
Cities and towns have taken over land that was once rain forest.

Clear-cutting is a farming practice in which land is cleared completely.
This process destroys **native** plant species. Another poor farming practice is
slash-and-burn farming. First, farmers harvest whatever wood they can. Then,
they burn the rest of the land to make way for crops or **grazing** animals.

All these activities end up killing plants and forcing animals to find a new
home. But where will these animals go? They are pushed into smaller and
smaller areas of land. There, they must compete for fewer resources.

RAIN FORESTS AT RISK

Many rain forests are at risk from mining. Rain forests contain many substances that are valuable to humans, such as gold, copper, and nickel. But mining operations release lots of waste. This harmful waste **pollutes** the air and water. It can harm—or even kill—plants and animals living nearby. The effects of **pollution** last for a long time. It is hard, or even impossible, to clean up polluted land.

One area especially at risk from mining and hunting is Sapo National Park. This park is in the African country of Liberia. It is the second largest rain forest in West Africa. But there are not enough park rangers to protect the park. People illegally hunt forest elephants and pygmy hippopotamus there. They clear the forest for grazing cattle and for growing crops. Some mine for gold and diamonds in the park. Many species that live in Sapo National Park are in danger, including chimpanzees and colobus monkeys.

Mines such as this one are responsible for polluting and destroying rain forests.

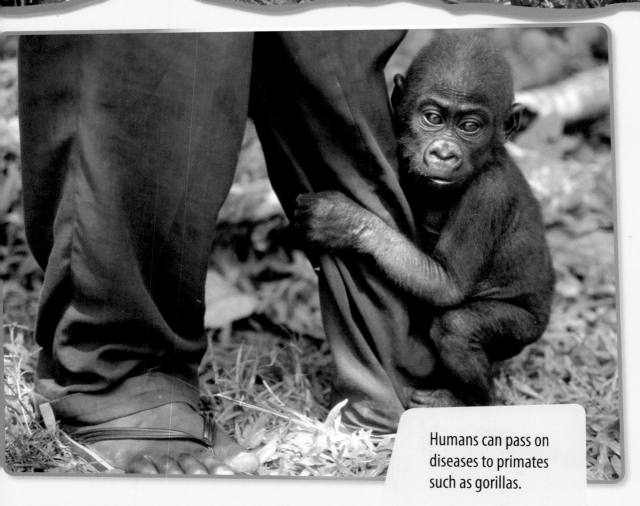

Humans can pass on diseases to primates such as gorillas.

DISAPPEARING PRIMATES

Hunting threatens many rain forest species. **Primates** such as chimps and lowland gorilla are now **endangered**. Fewer than 100,000 chimpanzees remain in the world. There are between 172,000 and 300,000 lowland gorillas, the type of gorilla that lives in **tropical** rain forests.

In parts of Africa, people illegally hunt primates for food. Their flesh is called bushmeat. The growth of towns and tourism also can affect the health of gorillas. People who come into contact with gorillas can pass on diseases to them.

Primates are our closest living relatives. Humans have much to learn from them. If they die out, we will lose a valuable link to ourselves.

A small area of rain forest was cleared for this cattle pasture.

HOPE FOR THE FUTURE

What will happen to the rain forests? Their fate is in human hands.

There is some good news. In some places, the rain forest is growing back. About 350,000 square kilometers (135,000 square miles) of rain forest is growing back around the world. Scientists have noted that the **canopy** fills in after about 15 years. This gives hope for the future.

The regrowth is due mainly to changing patterns of human life. In places such as Panama and parts of the Congo, more people are moving into cities. They are leaving behind farms grown on former rain forest land.

On these empty patches of land, the rain forest is taking over once more. Dense vegetation is filling in spaces where cattle once grazed or coffee once grew. Birds and other creatures are making a new home in this habitat.

But the new rain forest is not the same as it once was. The species that have died out can never come back. Old-growth rain forests (ones with very old trees) take in more carbon dioxide and give off more oxygen than regrown forests. Because of this, they are better at slowing global warming.

Still, it is hopeful news. More land means hope for many rain forest plants and animals. If the new rain forest is to thrive and grow, people must protect it. The future of the rain forests is up to us.

MADE IN THE RAIN FOREST

The rain forest is home to many plants with practical uses. These plants make our lives easier, tastier, and more fun. Rubber, Brazil nuts, coffee, chocolate, cinnamon, and vanilla are just a few rain forest products. Think about what life would be like without those things.

Parts of the Bunya Mountains rain forest in Queensland, Australia, that were once logged have regrown.

WHAT CAN YOU DO TO PROTECT RAIN FOREST FOOD CHAINS?

The rain forest supplies oxygen to the planet. It is home to many amazing **species** of plants and animals. If you or someone you love gets sick, rain forest plants might provide a treatment or cure. Today, the rain forest needs your help. What can you do to help protect it?

SUPPORT CONSERVATION GROUPS

People all over the world are working to preserve the rain forest. Support **conservation** groups that put money and research toward the problems facing the rain forest. Groups like the World Wildlife Fund work hard every day to prevent illegal hunting, fishing, and farming in the rain forest.

This zoo worker tries to give medicine to a sick orangutan that was illegally smuggled out of a rain forest.

It is important to support people who live in or near rain forests.

HELP ALL RAIN FOREST DWELLERS

Hippopotamuses and tapirs are not the only creatures that dwell in the rain forest. People make their home there, too. Millions of people across the world depend on rain forests for food and shelter. Sometimes these people do not have enough to eat. This drives them to hunt **endangered** animals or to chop down forests to grow crops or **graze** animals. It is important to help the people of the rain forest, too. Without their help, the rain forests will not survive.

FUEL FROM FUNGUS?

Gasoline is a major source of **pollution**. But it is hard to find a substitute. Now scientists have discovered one substance that might work. A type of tree **fungus** can turn plant matter into fuel. The fungus grows in the rain forests of Patagonia, at the tip of South America. Scientists think this might be a good source of renewable **energy**. Renewable energy is clean fuel from sources that do not run out, such as sunshine or wind. The fungus could grow in labs or in factories. It may help lessen our dependence on gasoline.

KIDS CAN MAKE A DIFFERENCE

In Manuel Antonio, Costa Rica, kids are working together to protect the rain forest. Kids Saving the Rainforest is a conservation group founded by two schoolchildren. In 1998 two nine-year-old girls decided to sell painted rocks to raise money for the local rain forest. More than 10 years later, the group is still going strong.

Today, the organization works to preserve rain forests and save endangered local monkeys. Kids Saving the Rainforest built an animal shelter to care for injured animals. The group releases the healthy animals back into the wild. Students who volunteer with the group help build monkey bridges. These bridges are built across roads in Manuel Antonio. They help local monkeys cross the road without getting hit by cars.

Students around the world can get involved in the group by raising money or asking local businesses to sponsor a monkey or rain forest tree.

Cards and letters from children in support of the Children's Eternal Rainforest in Costa Rica are displayed. This rain forest reserve is completely supported by children!

BUY SUSTAINABLE AND FAIR TRADE PRODUCTS

Ask your parents to buy rain forest products—such as bananas, chocolate, and coffee—that are grown sustainably. **Sustainable** products are grown in a way that does not harm the rain forest. Also, ask your parents to make sure your furniture and flooring comes from sustainable wood. Look for wood from certified sustainable forests.

Another label to look for is "fair trade." Fair trade products are made in ways that are less harmful to the environment. Fair trade also means the person who buys or grows the product is paid a fair price.

SPREAD THE WORD

Learn as much as you can about the amazing plants and creatures that live in the rain forest and take steps to protect them. Then share your knowledge with people you know. Together we can make a difference!

This woman harvests a fair trade coffee crop. It is important to buy fair trade products when possible.

TOP 10 THINGS YOU CAN DO TO PROTECT RAIN FORESTS

There are lots of things you can do to protect rain forest food chains and **habitats**. Here are 10 to start with:

1 Reduce, reuse, and recycle. Save trees. Use as little paper as possible. When you use paper, make sure it is recycled.

2 Write a letter to a **conservation** group to thank it for what it does. Or write to a group harming the rain forest and tell it to stop.

3 Hold a bake sale or raffle. Raise money for conservation groups such as the World Wildlife Fund or the Rainforest Conservation Fund.

4 Ask your parents to buy sustainably grown rain forest products. **Sustainable** products are grown or produced in ways that do not harm rain forests.

5 Buy **organic** food, if possible. **Pesticide** use harms rain forests and habitats everywhere.

6 At home or on vacation, don't feed the animals. Animals **adapt** to their habitat. Feeding them "people food" throws off their diet and could make them sick.

7 Let wild animals stay wild. Don't buy rain forest fish, monkeys, or birds to keep as pets. These animals belong in the rain forest. They are a key part of the rain forest food chain.

8 Support the people who live in the rain forest. They need your help, too! They depend on the rain forest for food and shelter.

9 Get smart. Learn as much as you can about rain forests. Tell your friends and family what you have learned.

10 Write an article in your school newspaper telling people how they can protect rain forests.

GLOSSARY

adapt develop a feature that helps a living thing survive. If a plant lives in the rain forest understory, then it is adapted to low levels of sunlight.

adaptation feature that helps a living thing survive. The poison that some frogs release from their skin is an adaptation that helps them scare off predators.

bacteria simple, one-celled living things. Bacteria help break down dead matter in the rain forest.

basin dip in the land

canopy top layer of the rain forest formed by treetops clustered together. Tall evergreen trees reaching up to 30 meters (100 feet) high form the canopy.

carnivore animal that eats only other animals. Jaguars and ocelots are the main rain forest carnivores.

chlorophyll chemical that makes plants green and helps them trap sunlight.

clear-cutting removal of all trees in an area

conservation preserving something, such as a natural resource. Some conservation groups help protect the rain forest.

consumer animal that cannot make its own food. Consumers eat plants or other animals, or both plants and animals.

decomposer living thing that breaks down dead plant and animal matter. Bacteria are the main rain forest decomposers.

emergent layer very tall trees that poke through the rain forest canopy. The emergent layer is above the canopy.

endangered at risk of dying out. Chimpanzees and lowland gorillas are endangered.

energy power needed to grow, move, and live

epiphyte plant that grows on tree trunks or branches and absorbs (takes in) nutrients from rainwater and air. Orchids, ferns, and bromeliads are all epiphytes.

extinction when all living things of a certain kind die out. Jaguars and ocelots are at risk of extinction.

feces solid waste from an animal (poo)

fungus (plural: **fungi**) group of rain forest decomposers that includes mushrooms. Fungus grows quickly in warm, wet rain forests.

global warming worldwide increase in air and ocean temperature. The loss of rain forest will worsen global warming.

graze eat grass and other green plants in a field or meadow

habitat place where organisms of the same kind live. Living things are adapted to their habitat.

herbivore living thing that eats only plants. Gorillas are rain forest herbivores.

mammal warm-blooded animal that produces milk to feed its young. Rats, gorillas, and humans are all mammals.

GLOSSARY

native plant or animal that lives in the place it is adapted to

nectar sugary substance made by plants

nutrient substance a living thing needs to live or grow

omnivore animal that eats both plants and animals. Humans are omnivores.

organic made in a natural way or containing only natural materials

organism living thing

pesticide poisonous chemical used to kill insects and other pests

photosynthesis process plants use to turn sunlight into energy

pollen small grains that are the male part of a flower

pollinate fertilize a plant by transferring pollen from another plant

pollination when a plant is fertilized by transferring pollen from another plant

pollute release harmful waste into the land, air, or water

pollution harmful waste

predator animal that eats another animal

prey animal that is eaten by another animal; also, when an animal pursues another animal to eat it

primary consumer animal that consumes producers (plants)

primate group of mammals that share certain features, such as hands that grasp and well-formed brains. Monkeys, gorillas, chimpanzees, and humans are all primates.

producer organism that can make its own food, using energy from the Sun. Plants are producers.

scavenger animal that feeds on dead matter

secondary consumer predator, or animal that feeds on a primary consumer

species type of plant or animal. Rain forests are home to thousands of plant and animal species.

sustainable something that is done in a way that does not deplete resources. Sustainable products are raised or produced in a way that does not harm the environment.

tertiary consumer third-level consumer, or animal that feeds on animals that eat other animals. "Big cats" are the top tertiary consumers.

tropical having to do with a region of high temperatures and heavy rainfall. Rain forests are found in tropical areas of the world.

understory area below the canopy in a rain forest. Smaller trees, plants, and shrubs grow in the understory.

vegetation plant life. Rain forests contain many kinds of vegetation.

FIND OUT MORE

BOOKS

Aloian, Molly, and Bobbie Kalman. *A Rainforest Habitat* (*Introducing Habitats*). New York: Crabtree, 2007.

Ruurs, Margriet. *My School in the Rain Forest: How Children Attend School Around the World*. Honesdale, Pa.: Boyds Mills, 2009.

Tagliaferro, Linda. *Explore the Tropical Rain Forest* (*Fact Finders*). North Mankato, Minn.: Capstone, 2007.

WEBSITES

www.rainforest-alliance.org/education
Visit the website of the Rainforest Alliance for fun facts, stories, and projects dealing with the plants and animals of the rain forest.

www.kidssavingtherainforest.org/
Kids Saving the Rainforest, a nonprofit group based in Costa Rica, links students with rain forest conservation projects.

www.arborday.org/programs/rainforest/kids.cfm
The Arbor Day Foundation runs this website, which offers information on rain forests, virtual tours, and advice on contacting local TV and radio stations.

www.pbs.org/journeyintoamazonia/explorer.html
Play "Amazon Explorer" and learn the secrets of the Amazon rain forest from scientists at the American Museum of Natural History.

FURTHER RESEARCH

Choose a topic from this book you'd like to research further. Do you live near a rain forest you would like to know more about? Or is there a faraway rain forest you think is exotic? Was there a creature in this book you find interesting? Is there something harming rain forest food chains you'd like to know more about putting a stop to? Visit your local library to find out more information.

INDEX

acacia plants 17
adaptation 9, 21, 28
African forest elephants 30, 36
African rain forest 8, 22, 30–31, 36, 37
agoutis 16
Amazon rain forest 4, 8, 15, 19, 28–29
Amazon River 8
anacondas 20
ants 17, 25

bacteria 4, 16, 26
bandicoots 20
bats 18, 19, 21
birds 4, 16, 18, 20, 21, 23, 28, 29, 32, 38
blue morpho butterfly 19
bonobos 30
bromeliads 15
"bushmeat" 37
butterflies 16, 19, 28

canopy 9, 12, 16, 18, 25, 38
capybaras 16
carbon dioxide 12, 34, 39
carnivores 6, 23, 32
chimpanzees 22, 23, 30, 36, 37
chlorophyll 12
clear-cutting 35, 36, 41
climate 4, 8, 26, 27
coatimundis 20
Congo River 8, 30, 32
conservation groups 40, 42
consumers 6, 12, 16, 20, 22, 23, 32

decomposers 4, 6, 24–27
diseases 25, 27, 29, 34, 37

emergent layer 12, 18
endangered species 23, 34, 37, 41, 42
epiphytes 15

farming 29, 31, 33, 35, 36, 38, 40, 41
"flying" animals 21, 33
food webs 7, 22
forest floor 4, 9, 12, 15, 16, 20, 29
fungi 25, 26, 27, 30, 41

global warming 34, 39
gorillas 22, 30, 31, 37
grazing 35, 36, 38, 41

habitat loss 15, 19, 23, 33, 35
habitats 8, 9, 28
herbivores 6, 16, 31.
hummingbirds 18
hunting 23, 36, 37, 40, 41

insects 4, 15, 16, 17, 18, 20, 21, 22, 29, 32

jaguars 23, 29

king vultures 25

lemurs 32
logging 33, 35

mammals 20, 22, 30
mandrills 22
medicines 15, 29, 34, 40
mining 36

Niger River 8

ocelots 23
okapis 30
old-growth rain forests 39
omnivores 6, 20, 22
orangutans 14, 32
orchids 9, 15
oxygen 34, 40

photosynthesis 12
pitcher plants 32
poison dart frogs 29

pollination 18, 19
pollution 36, 41
prey 6, 20, 21, 23, 29
primary consumers 6, 16–19, 20, 22.
primates 14, 22, 23, 29, 30, 31, 36, 37, 42
producers 6, 12–15, 16, 24, 30, 32
pygmy marmosets 29

rainfall 8
renewable energy 41
reptiles 18, 20, 21, 22, 29, 33
roads 31, 35, 42
rodents 16, 20, 21, 23, 30
roots 13, 14, 20, 22, 30

Sapo National Park 36
scavengers 6, 25
secondary consumers 6, 20–23, 32.
slash-and-burn farming 35
sloths 5, 17, 29
soil 4, 14, 24
Southeast Asian rain forest 8, 21, 32–33, 35
strangler figs 13
sustainable products 43

tertiary consumers 23
toucans 4, 18
tourism 37
trees 9, 12, 13, 14, 15, 16, 17, 19, 21, 25, 27, 29, 30, 32, 39, 42

understory 9, 12, 19, 20, 29, 32

vines 9, 14

wastes 16, 24, 26, 36
World Wildlife Fund 40